I0824508

Level Up Gaming

LORI DITTMER

BLACK RABBIT BOOKS

Bolt is published by Black Rabbit Books
P.O. Box 227, Mankato, Minnesota, 56002.
www.blackrabbitbooks.com

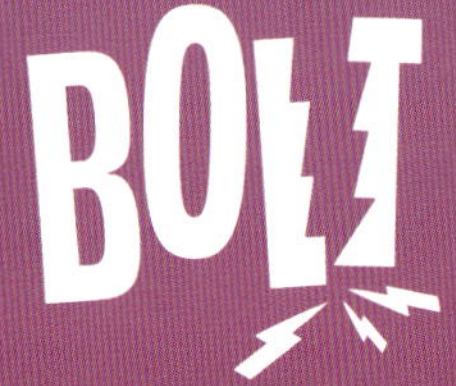

Alissa Thielges, editor; Rhea Magaro, designer and photo researcher

Library of Congress Cataloging-in-Publication Data
Names: Dittmer, Lori author
Title: Level up Super Smash Bros / Lori Dittmer.
Description: Mankato, MN: Black Rabbit Books, [2026] | Series: Level up gaming | Includes bibliographical references and index. | Audience: Ages 8-12 | Audience: Grades 4-6
Identifiers: LCCN 2025017487 (print) | LCCN 2025017488 (ebook) | ISBN 9781645824817 library binding | ISBN 9781645824893 ebook
Subjects: LCSH: Super Smash Bros. (Game)—Juvenile literature
Classification: LCC GV1469.35.S98 D58 2026 (print) | LCC GV1469.35.S98 (ebook) | DDC 794.8—dc23/eng/20250618
LC record available at https://lccn.loc.gov/2025017487
LC ebook record available at https://lccn.loc.gov/2025017488

Printed in China

Image Credits

Dreamstime/Yuriy Nedopekin, 25; Nintendo, cover, 1, 3, 4-5, 6, 7, 9, 10, 11, 12, 13, 14, 15, 16, 17, 18-19, 20, 21, 22, 23, 24, 26, 27, 28, 29, 31, 32; Shutterstock/NextMarsMedia, 23, Vina amelia, cover.

CONTENTS

CHAPTER 1

FINAL KNOCKOUT

A *Super Smash Bros*. battle is almost over. Kirby floats around the stage. Mario jumps and jabs. He throws a fireball! Kirby dodges it. Then Kirby inhales. A red hat appears on his head. He just copied Mario's move! Now he throws a fireball at Mario. Mario flies off the stage. Kirby wins!

Kirby and Mario were two of the first characters in *Super Smash Bros*.

TIMELINE OF GAMES

Smash Beginnings

Super Smash Bros. is a **platform fighter** game. Fighters try to knock opponents off a stage. The last one left on the stage is the winner. Players chose their fighters. These are popular characters from other games. Mario could fight Pikachu. Donkey Kong could face Yoshi. There are many options!

CHAPTER 2

GETTING STARTED

Fighters battle on a stage. Each stage looks like a scene from a character's game. Early games had just a few stages. Now there are more than 100!

Each stage has **hazards**. Launchers toss fighters into the air. A moving camera might knock down a fighter. Stage bosses are strong enemies. They show up to add more challenges.

STAGE HAZARDS

moving platforms
blasts
acid
lava

Choosing a Fighter

First, pick a fighter. There are more than 80 to choose from. But each game starts with a few. Players must beat classic **mode** with each starting fighter. Then they can unlock more fighters. For example, finishing as Mario may unlock Sonic.

Sonic is the fastest fighter in the game.

STARTING FIGHTERS

Super Smash Bros. Ultimate has eight starting fighters.

FOX

SAMUS

YOSHI

LINK

PIKACHU

DONKEY KONG

KIRBY

MARIO

Stage bosses have hit point meters. They are strong enemies!

Taking Damage

Each player has a **damage** meter. It shows how much a fighter has been hurt. This meter starts at zero. It goes up as fighters get hurt. Damage weakens them. Weaker players fly farther when hit. They are more likely to fall off the stage. Then it's game over.

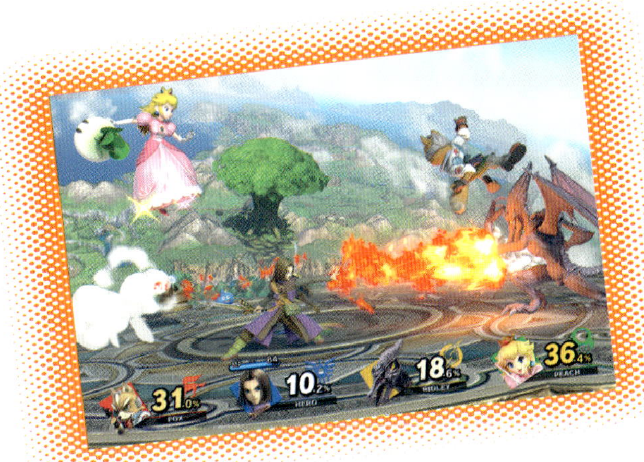

CHAPTER 3

LEVELING UP

All fighters can run, jump, and punch. Each move has a cooldown period. After a move, the fighter must wait before hitting again. This leaves them open to an attack. Skilled players learn each fighter's moves. They level up by making **combos**. These make attacks stronger.

Each fighter also has a special move. Pikachu's is Thunder Jolt.

Shadow
slows down fighters

Ashley
creates an area of darkness

Knuckles
spins and hits fighters

Grabbing Items

Items pop up on stage. They can help you win. Some items heal. Others give special powers. Break a smash ball to gain a strong attack. Throw a banana peel to trip another fighter. Poké Balls have Pokémon in them. An assist trophy brings another character into the fight. They will help you in the battle.

CHAPTER 4

MASTERING THE SMASH

The best players make a plan. They think ahead. They guess where an enemy will land. Then they aim an attack at that spot.

A battle lasts a few minutes. But completing the story can take hours. Players battle several fighters. Then they must beat the bosses to end the game.

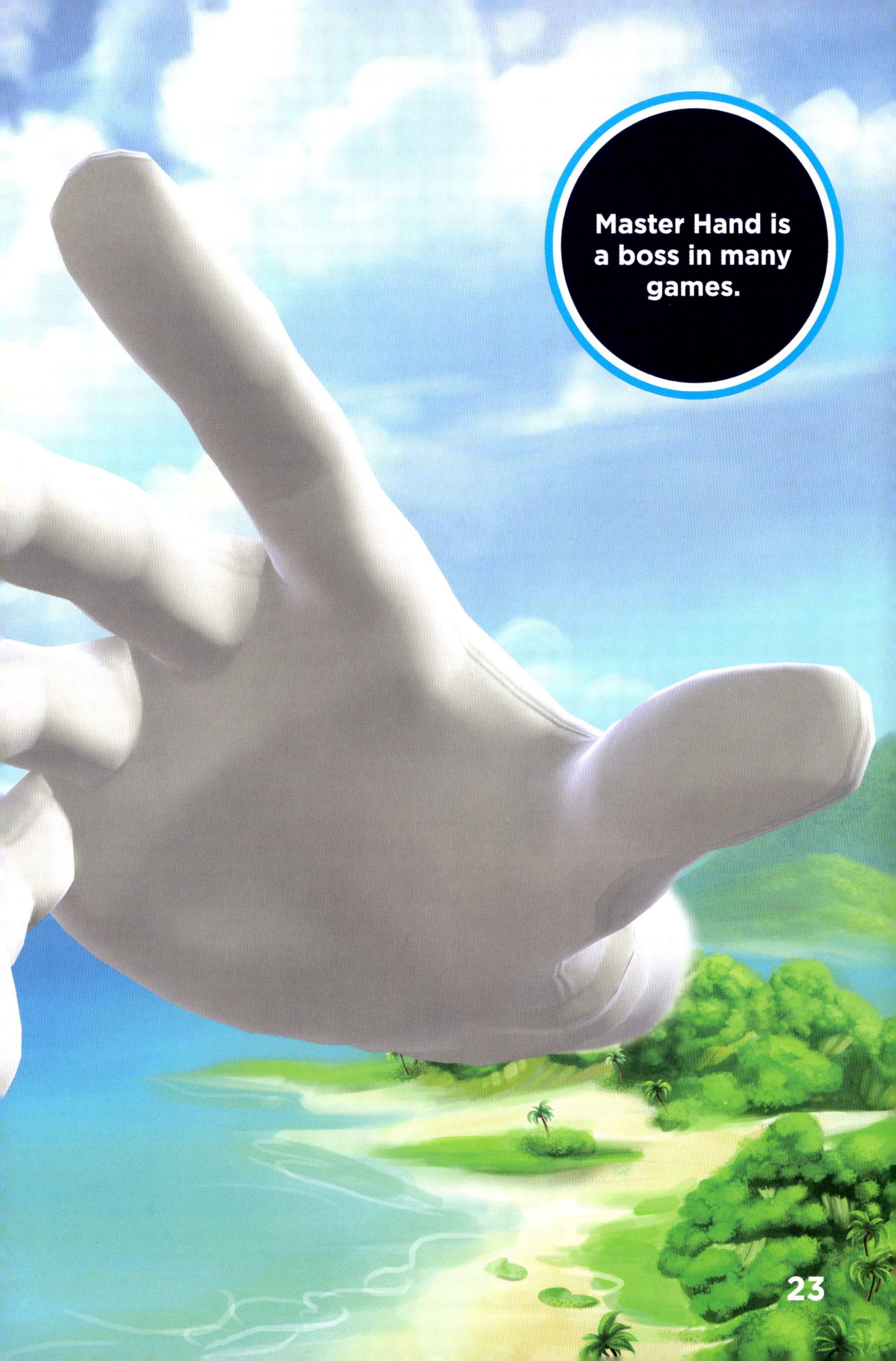

Master Hand is a boss in many games.

Professional Esport

Super Smash Bros. is also an **esport**. Supernova is one of the biggest events. It takes place over four days each year. Pros show off their skills. Another big event is GENESIS. It has **tournaments** for lots of games. In 2024, GENESIS held events for *Melee* and *Ultimate*.

Mew2King
(Jason Zimmerman)
Often seen as the overall GOAT smasher.

MkLeo
(Leonardo Pérez)
Earned about $300,000 playing pro.
GOAT player for the *Ultimate* game.

"King of Smash"
(Ken Hoang)
Skilled player in early 2000s.

Sparg0
(Edgar Valdez)
#1 player today in the *Ultimate* game.

Wizzrobe
(Justin Hallett)
Top player in the *Melee* and *Ultimate* games.

An Exciting Crossover

Super Smash Bros. is a fighting game like no other. Each new game adds more familiar names and items. The stages keep getting better. Players can have fun. Or they can study the game. They can learn every move. They make combos. The best fighters are the last ones standing!

GLOSSARY

combo (KOM-boh)—a combination of different things

damage (DAM-ij)—physical harm done to something or someone's body

esport (EE-spawrt)—competitive video gaming

hazard (HAZ-erd)—something that makes playing a game more difficult

mode (MOHD)—a set of rules within a game that changes how it is played

platform fighter (PLAT-fawrm FAHY-ter)—a type of fighting game where characters can move freely in a 2D space

tournament (TUR-nuh-muhnt)—a series of matches between several teams, ending in one winner

BOOKS

Gregory, Josh. *Starter Guide to Super Smash Bros.* Ann Arbor, MI: Cherry Lake Publishing, 2024.

Rusick, Jessica. *Super Smash Bros.* North Mankato, MN: Checkerboard Library, 2022.

Storm, Marysa. *Fighting Games.* Mankato, MN: Black Rabbit Books, 2026.

WEBSITES

How to Smash
www.smashbros.com/en_US/howtoplay/index.html

Super Smash Bros. Ultimate Beginner Strategies
play.nintendo.com/news-tips/tips-tricks/super-smash-bros-ultimate-beginner-strategies

Super Smash Bros. Ultimate Guide
www.ign.com/wikis/super-smash-bros-ultimate

INDEX